THIS BOOK BELONGS TO

Calym Kennedy

SCOOBY-DOO'S NUMBER 1 FAN!

£6.99

D1423012

SCOOBY-DOO!

SCOOBY-DOO

Welcome!

Like, hey dudes, welcome to the Scooby-Doo Annual 2006! It's the place to be if you love all things to do with the Mystery, Inc. gang. There are mad monsters, ghastly ghouls and spooky surprises packed onto every page. Check out the spine-tingling Scooby adventures, create your own fun Scooby-Doo craft projects and tackle the spookerific quizzes and puzzles.

So grab your Scooby Snacks and join the gang for plenty of mystery and mayhem. Scooby-dooby-doo!

CONTENTS

SHAGGY

DAPHNE

FRED

VELMA

IT JUST DOESN'T MAKE ANY -- OH, NO.

MORNING, SILVERS. LOST ANYTHING IMPORTANT TODAY? OH, OF COURSE NOT. YOU DON'T *SHIP* ANYTHING IMPORTANT. *HA, HA, HA!*

VERY FUNNY.

KIDS, THIS IS FRED X. DEAL. HE RUNS SHIP SHAPE EXPRESS, THE --

THE *FASTEST-IF-IT-MUST-GET-THERE-BEFORE-YOU-COULD-DELIVER-IT-YOURSELF* COURIER SERVICE IN THE COUNTY!

IN FACT, *THREE* MORE SHOPS HAVE DECIDED TO DO THEIR SHIPPING WITH ME. SEE, NOTHING STOPS *MY* PEOPLE, NOT EVEN *GHOSTS.*

GHOST? WHAT'S THAT ABOUT A *GHOST?* DID HE STRIKE *AGAIN?*

EXIT

NO, NO, MS. WHYTE. NOT AT ALL.

I SHOULD HOPE NOT. NOT WITH THAT *PACKAGE* COMING --

KIDS, MS. WHYTE HERE OWNS *BAUBLES AND BANGLES,* THE TOWN'S MOST ELEGANT JEWELRY STORE.

YES, IT IS, AND I NEED TO TALK WITH YOU IMMEDIATELY.

THEN MAYBE WE *ALL* SHOULD LEAVE.

YES... MAYBE WE SHOULD. ADIOS FOR NOW!

MR. SILVERS HAS MAJOR TROUBLES. I HOPE WE CAN HELP!

LIKE, IT'S EASIER TO HELP ON A FULL STOMACH! SO LET'S FIND AN ALL-YOU-CAN-EAT CHUCK WAGON BUFFET AND --

NO TIME. WE NEED TO MOVE FAST. VELMA CAN DO SOME RESEARCH...

"...AND MEANWHILE, THE REST OF US WILL GO POSTAL GHOST HUNTING -- *TONIGHT!*"

LIKE, SCOOB, THIS IS *TORTURE!*

WE GET TO DRIVE THIS MAIL TRUCK AS A DECOY, BUT WE CAN'T TOUCH ANY OF THOSE FOOD GOODIES IN TONIGHT'S MAIL DELIVERY. *CANDY, COOKIES, CRUMB CAKE!*

REAH! ROOKIES!

WHAT COULD BE *WORSE?*

YEEE HA, HA, HA!!!

RHAT ROULD!

IT'S MINE, MINE!!!

WHAT? THE COOKIES, OR THE CRUMB CAKE?

HANG ON, GUYS! WE'LL TRAP HIM BETWEEN US!

THE MYSTERY MACHINE

LOOK OUT!

US MAIL

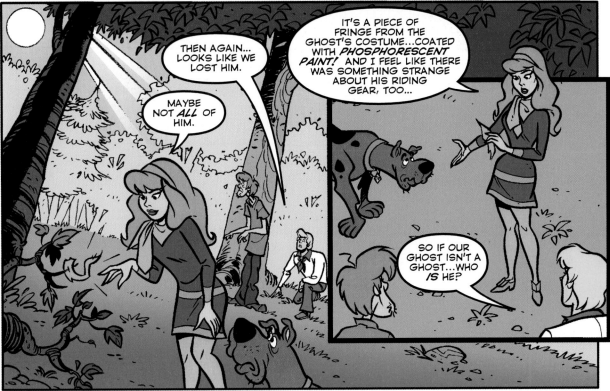

CONTINUED ON PAGE 13

YOU WILL NEED!

Thick card, scissors, a bowl of PVA glue mixed with water, newspaper, kitchen paper, sticky pads, a bottle of red paint, paints and a paintbrush.

1

Draw and cut out a rectangle from card. Snip into two sides of the card with scissors so that it looks like a rough plank of wood. Cover the rectangle with a layer of torn-up newspaper dipped in the PVA glue mixture and leave it to dry.

2

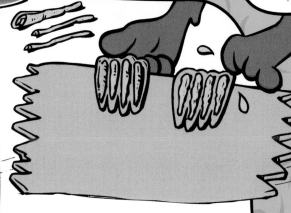

Draw and cut out two creepy hand shapes from card. Pad them out using scrunched-up kitchen paper and PVA glue. Stick them to the top of your board.

3

Paint the sign brown to look like wood. Add streaks of different shades of brown to create the wood texture. Paint the hands green with black claws.

4

Sketch out your message with a pencil. Then squirt red paint straight from the bottle to spell out each word. Prop up the sign to make the red paint drip down the board. When you are happy with how it looks, lay the board flat to dry.

5

Add some creepy crawlies with a thin paintbrush and black paint. Once it is dry, fix the sign to your door with sticky pads. Let's see who's brave enough to enter your room now!

SCOOBY WHO?

Get to know the Mystery, Inc. gang with these crazy-but-true Scooby facts!

THE GROOVY GANG!

MYSTERY, INC. MEMBER 01

SCOOBY-DOO

Scooby-Doo's full name is Scoobert-Doo and he is a Great Dane. He is seven years old and he lives in a kennel in Shaggy's back yard.

MYSTERY, INC. MEMBER 02

SHAGGY

Shaggy's real name is Norville Rogers and he is the oldest member of the gang. Shaggy loves food and one of his hobbies is inventing crazy pizza toppings!

MYSTERY, INC. MEMBER 03

DAPHNE

Daphne is the daughter of a millionaire. Her nickname is Danger Prone Daphne because she is always getting caught by spooks!

MYSTERY, INC. MEMBER 04

FRED

Freddie is the leader of Mystery, Inc. and he always leads the way when there is a monster to be caught. He spends his spare time inventing monster traps.

MYSTERY, INC. MEMBER 05

VELMA

Velma is the youngest member of the gang. She is super-brainy and enjoys translating ancient texts in her spare time.

FAST FACTS!

Velma is always losing her glasses so Shaggy carries a spare pair for her.

One of the freakiest villains that the gang has taken on was a Living Burger!

The gang live in Coolsville and one of their favourite hang-outs is called The Malt Shop. Shaggy reckons it serves the biggest and best pizzas in town!

The Mystery Machine weighs 2.6 tonnes and has a top speed of 60 mph.

If a ghost pops up while Scooby is asleep, his ears will tap him on the head to wake him up.

Fred is really brave but he admits that he is scared of creepy-crawly spiders!

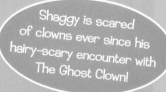

Shaggy is scared of clowns ever since his hairy-scary encounter with The Ghost Clown!

Shaggy is terrified of ghosts, shadows, bats and all things scary. Even his squeaking shoes scare this groovy dude! Zoinks!

SQUEAK! SQUEAK!

MEANWHILE, AT THE *WAILING DAILY NEWS*...

SEEMS EVEN THE POLICE ARE BAFFLED BY THIS GHOST.

BUT I'VE LEARNED A FEW THINGS ABOUT OUR CLIENT.. AND ABOUT OUR MAIN SUSPECT.

RING RING

HEY, VELMA. WE'RE ON OUR WAY BACK WITH OUR FIRST CLUE. HAVE YOU FOUND ANYTHING?

I'M NOT SURE. BECAUSE THE TOWN IS SMALL, MR. DEAL HAS TO TAKE AWAY SOME OF THE POST OFFICE'S CUSTOMERS, OR HE CAN'T STAY IN BUSINESS.

AND THE SAME GOES FOR MS. WHYTE. HER MERCHANDISE IS TOO EXPENSIVE FOR THIS TOWN. BUT SHE'S GOT SOME BIG JEWELRY DEAL COOKING THIS WEEK THAT MIGHT SAVE HER.

HOW DOES THAT TIE IN WITH THE POSTAL GHOST?

The GAZ...
Busine...

City Dude Comes West

Whyte Makes Hush-Hush Deal With Deal

I'M NOT SURE. BUT...SILVERS COULD ALSO BE A SUSPECT. HE OWNS AND RIDES A HORSE!

Sivers Wins Again!

"I SAW A PICTURE OF HIM AND MS. WHYTE AT A HORSE SHOW. MEET ME AT THE POST OFFICE AND I'LL TELL YOU ALL ABOUT IT."

WELL, WE DO KNOW THE GHOST ISN'T REAL. WE HAVE PART OF HIS COSTUME!

WHAT'S GOING ON OUT HERE?

AND NOW WE KNOW THAT MR. SILVERS ISN'T THE POSTAL GHOST.

THAT MEANS THE GHOST IS MR. DEAL!

THEN LET'S TELL THE SHERIFF. THE GHOST HAS TO BE STOPPED TONIGHT!

WHAT'S SO SPECIAL ABOUT TONIGHT?

NOTHING. UH, I MEAN...

THERE IS SOMETHING SPECIAL, MR. SILVERS! EVEN THE GHOST MENTIONED IT. AND I BET IT HAS SOMETHING TO DO WITH MS. WHYTE'S BIG JEWELRY DEAL.

YOU REALLY SHOULD TELL US ABOUT IT...

..."BEFORE IT'S TOO LATE."

YEEE HA, HA, HA!!!

US MAIL

WHOOP, WHOOP, WAHOOOOOOO!

OR SHOULD I SAY, *HER?*

I -- I DON'T UNDERSTAND!

I DIDN'T EITHER, UNTIL I NOTICED *MS. WHYTE* WAS ALSO PICTURED IN THE HORSE SHOW ARTICLE, AS THE *RUNNER-UP!*

THEN *I* POINTED OUT THE GHOST WAS USING AN *ENGLISH* SADDLE, NOT A *WESTERN* ONE...

...JUST LIKE THE ONE *HER* HORSE HAD IN THE PHOTO!

THEN WE LEARNED ABOUT HOW SHE'D ARRANGED TO SELL SOMEONE'S VALUABLE *DIAMOND RING* FOR THEM.

MR. SILVERS TOLD US THAT THE RING WAS BEING SECRETLY SHIPPED THROUGH THE MAIL. IT'S A TRICK A LOT OF JEWELRY MERCHANTS USE.

MS. WHYTE PLANNED TO STEAL THE RING AS THE GHOST, SELL IT SOMEPLACE ELSE, AND RUN OFF WITH THE MONEY!

I'D BE SUNNING IN THE BAHAMAS TOMORROW IF IT WEREN'T FOR YOU *MEDDLING KIDS!*

WELL, THAT CASE SURE WORKED UP AN APPETITE!

GOOD, BECAUSE I ARRANGED TO HAVE A BIG DINNER SPREAD WAITING FOR US BACK AT THE POST OFFICE.

BUT WE HAVE TO STOP OFF AT THE SHERIFF'S, THEN THE BARN, AND --

CAN'T KEEP THE FOOD WAITING THAT LONG. *BYE, BYE* SILVERS!

ROOBY, ROOOOOOOO!

HA HA HA HA HA

THE END

17

JEEPERS, IT'S THE CREEPER!

He crawls, he creeps, and he's one of the scariest villains that the gang has ever met! Have a go at drawing your own picture of The Creeper.

1

Start by drawing two overlapping circles for his body. Sketch in the position of his head - use the steps opposite to help you. Add two small circles at the top for his shoulders and two more underneath for his knees. Sketch in lines for his legs.

2

Draw a curved line from his upper body to the ground for his arm. Now add a circle for each hand and sketch in the position of his fingers. Start to build up the shape of his feet.

3

Start building up the shape of his arms and legs. Draw lines to give some shape to his coat and trousers.

4

Once you are happy with the shape, use a thin black pen to draw over your finished outline. Rub out any unwanted lines and colour your finished picture in.

1

2

3

Try drawing your own Creeper picture in the scene below.

Start with two overlapping egg shapes for The Creeper's face. Draw in his eyes — make one a bit bigger than the other! Now sketch in the shape of his hair and ears, then add his nose. Draw in a diagonal line for the position of his mouth and build it up by adding the shape of the lips.

TUNNEL of LOVE

HORTENSE, YOU'RE SO *BEAUTIFUL* IN THIS LIGHT...

WE'RE IN THE *DARK*, MELVIN.

HORTENSE! WHAT'S *THAT?!*

I DON'T KNOW-- BUT ITS TIMING SURE IS *GOOD!*

AAAAAA

THEY'RE EVERYWHERE!

AAAAAAAAA!!!

GOOP ON THE LOOSE

SCREAMS! FROM THE *TUNNEL OF LOVE!*

IF YOU DON'T LIKE SCREAMS, *DON'T* ASK ME TO DITCH MY PIZZA!

C'MON, GANG! DITCH THE FOOD AND LET'S GO!

TUNNEL

PIZZA

writer: RURIK TYLER
penciller: JOE STATON
inker: ANDREW PEPOY
letters: JOHN COSTANZA
colors: PAUL BECTON
assists: HARVEY RICHARDS
edits: DANA KURTIN

HI! CAN WE HELP?

HEY! YOU KIDS ARE THE *MYSTERY SOLVERS* WHO DRIVE THAT VAN... THE *UHM...RIDDLE ROD*, RIGHT?

YOU MEAN THE *MYSTERY MACHINE*. YES, THAT'S US.

THANK GOODNESS YOU'RE HERE! TONIGHT IS OUR *BIG* OPENING DAY FIREWORKS DISPLAY. WE CAN'T HAVE ANY GIANT--WHAT?--

--RUNNING AROUND.

PINK MONSTERS!

BUMP!

YOU KIDS SOLVE THIS MYSTERY AND I'LL GIVE YOU A REWARD. DON'T LET THIS INTERRUPT THE FIREWORKS DISPLAY, GOT IT?

SO WHAT HAPPENED?

LIKE WE TOLD MR. TONKLIN, WE WERE SITTING IN THE RIDE WHEN THESE *GIANT PINK MONSTERS* ATTACKED US.

FRIENDLY GUY..., SORT OF.

THIS IS YOUR DOG, RIGHT? HE ON THE CASE ALREADY?

LIKE, HE PROBABLY JUST SMELLS SOME FOOD.

SNIF SNIF!

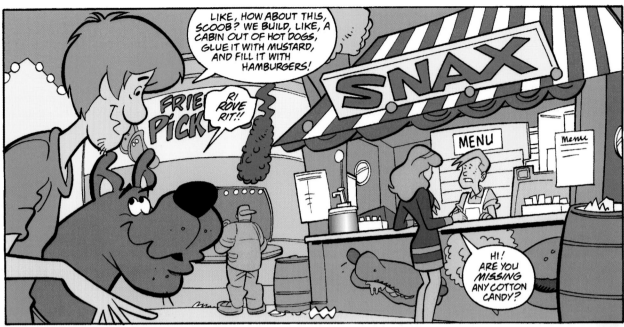

LIKE, HOW ABOUT THIS, SCOOB? WE BUILD, LIKE, A CABIN OUT OF HOT DOGS, GLUE IT WITH MUSTARD, AND FILL IT WITH HAMBURGERS!

FRIE PICKL

RI ROVE RIT!!

S.NAX

MENU

Menu

HI! ARE YOU MISSING ANY COTTON CANDY?

I WISH I KNEW! THIS PLACE IS A WRECK!

C'MON IN AND TAKE A LOOK YOURSELF.

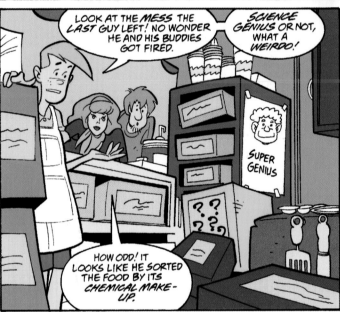

LOOK AT THE MESS THE LAST GUY LEFT! NO WONDER HE AND HIS BUDDIES GOT FIRED.

SCIENCE GENIUS OR NOT, WHAT A WEIRDO!

SUPER GENIUS

HOW ODD! IT LOOKS LIKE HE SORTED THE FOOD BY ITS CHEMICAL MAKE-UP.

SUDDENLY...

TWACK!

THE COTTON CANDY MONSTERS!

NO CANDY'S BOSSING ME AROUND!

LET'S GET HIM!

WUMP!

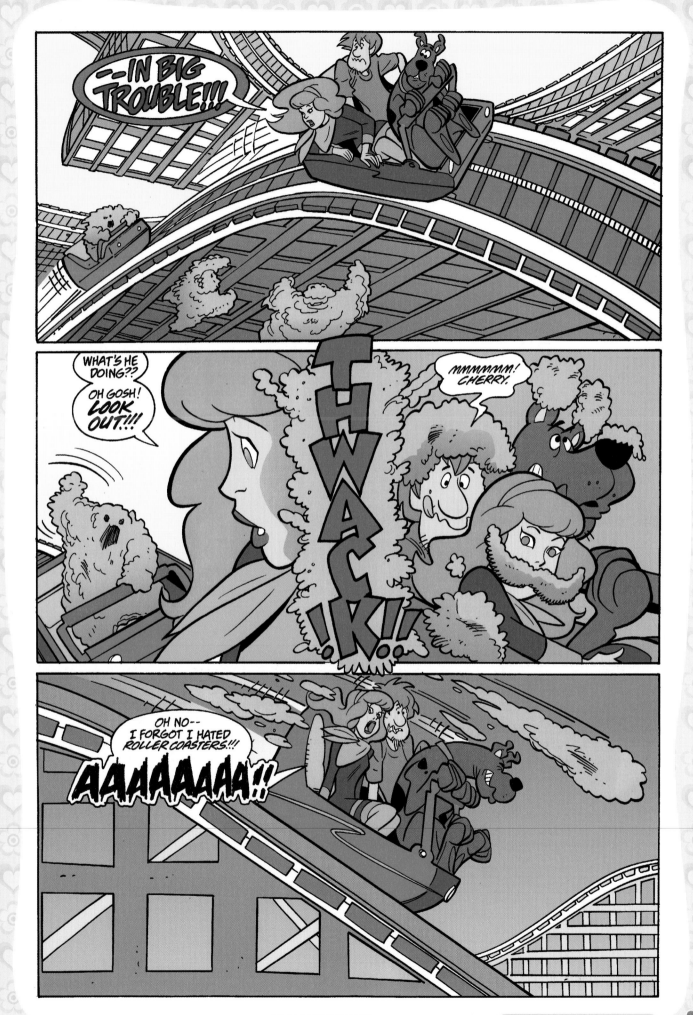

CONTINUED ON PAGE 28

BOOK IT UP!

Scooby up your book shelf with these groovy bookends! They look great and they are really fun to make.

SIDE VIEW! →

YOU WILL NEED: Thick card, two square cardboard boxes, a cardboard tube, scissors, a bowl of PVA glue diluted with water, sticky tape, two balloons, kitchen paper, pencil, split peas or rice, newspaper, paints and paintbrush.

1

Cut four oval shapes from card to make Scooby's feet. Cut the cardboard tube into four sections and tape one onto each foot.

2

Fill each of the legs with split peas or rice to give them some weight. Now tape two legs firmly to each box.

3

Roll up some kitchen paper into a sausage shape for Scooby's tail. Tape it in position.

4

Partly blow up the balloons and cover them with two layers of torn-up newspaper dipped in the glue mixture. Once they are dry, pop them. Cut a hole in one balloon and fit the other inside it to make a head shape.

5

Cut a strip of card and bend it into a circle to make Scooby's neck. Tape the head onto it and add card ears and a nose made from a ball of kitchen paper.

6

Cover each of the Scooby halves with 2-3 layers of PVA glue and torn-up newspaper and leave it to dry. Paint your bookends Scooby brown and add a blue and yellow collar. Once they are dry, your bookends are ready to use!

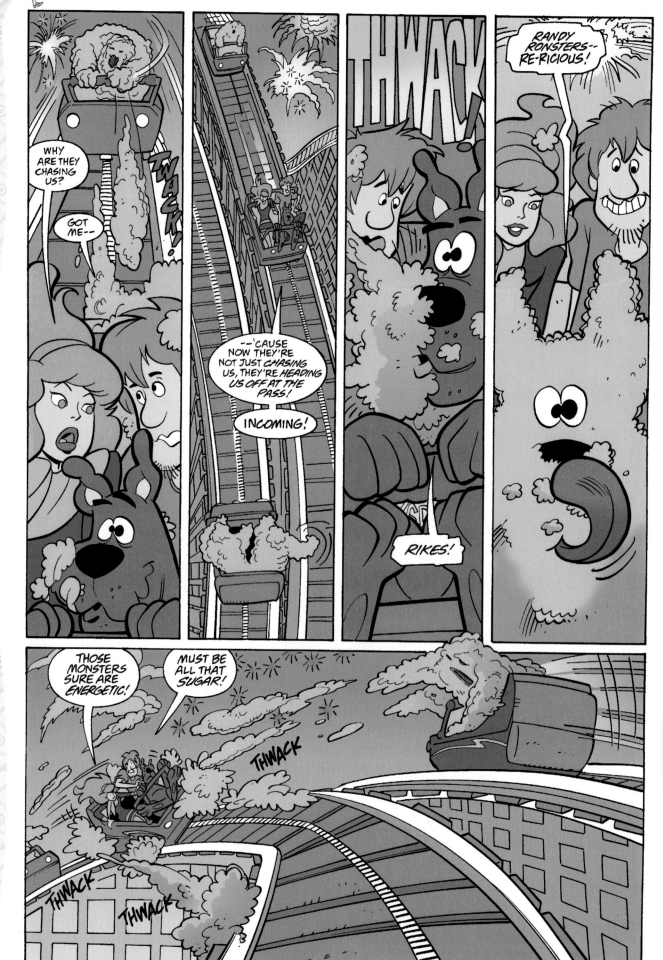

I'M GLAD YOU'RE SHOWING SOME SENSE, SHAGGY. I WAS SURE YOU'D BE EATING THAT FLYING CANDY!

WELL, FIRST WE HAVE TO CATCH SOME!

SHAGGY!

YES! GOT--

--IT?!

SHAGGY, GET BACK HERE!

ZOINKS!

ROLD, RON!

THIS IS NO TIME FOR TAKE-OUT!

HOW BRAVE ARE YOU?

Are you brave, bold and always ready to beat up a baddie? Or are you spooked by the dark and as scaredy as Shaggy? Find out with this cool quiz!

1

You spot something green and furry lurking under your bed. What do you think?

a) Zoinks! It's a green monster! Gemme outta here!

b) Aha, that's where my missing pair of green socks got to.

c) Cool! It could be a monster, it's time to investigate!

2

Which book would you read before you go to sleep?

a) 'Aliens to Zombies – a Monster History'

b) 'Sweet Dreams – how to dream of Cakes and Cookies'

c) 'Terrifying Tales to Make you Shiver'

3

Fred is setting a trap for a Mud Monster and you are the bait. Whaddya say?

a) Let me at it, I'll teach it a thing or two about being scary!

b) What a fascinating opportunity to get up close to a rare monster.

c) Like, no way mister! I'm, like, allergic to mud... and monsters!

4

You and the gang are investigating a haunted house. A hand grabs your shoulder, what happens next?

a) You grab it, get it in an arm lock and tie that bad guy up!

b) You shout "Quick, gang, the monster is over here!"

c) You say "I'm sorry Mr. Hand, am I in your way?" and then run for it!

5

It's the midnight hour, you're tucked up in bed and you hear a noise. Eeek! What was it?

a) Just the water pipes clunking, silly!

b) You don't know but you hide in the cupboard just in case!

c) Definitely a hobgoblin stomping up the stairs. How cool is that?

HOW DID YOU DO?

1 A – 3, B – 5, C – 10

2 A – 5, B – 3, C – 10

3 A – 10, B – 5, C – 3

4 A – 10, B – 5, C – 3

5 A – 5, B – 3, C – 10

SCAREDY DOG!

0-20 points

Jinkies, were you brave enough to make it to the end of the quiz? Nerves of steel are not really your thing and scaredy could be your middle name. That's okay though, Scooby and Shaggy reckon it's the best way to be!

BRAVE AND BOLD!

21-35 points

Cool, calm and totally brave – that's you! You don't scare easily and you use your brains to keep you out of the way of monsters. Mystery, Inc. could definitely use you on the mystery-solving team!

FEARLESS!

36-50 points

Ghosts and ghouls? Pah! An army of goop monsters? Not a problem! You're so brave that you love the idea of anything scary. Beware though, it's best to think before you jump straight in. That way you won't get squished by a Sludge Ghoul - yeuck!

CREEPY CROSSWORD!

Use your detective skills to solve this monster crossword!

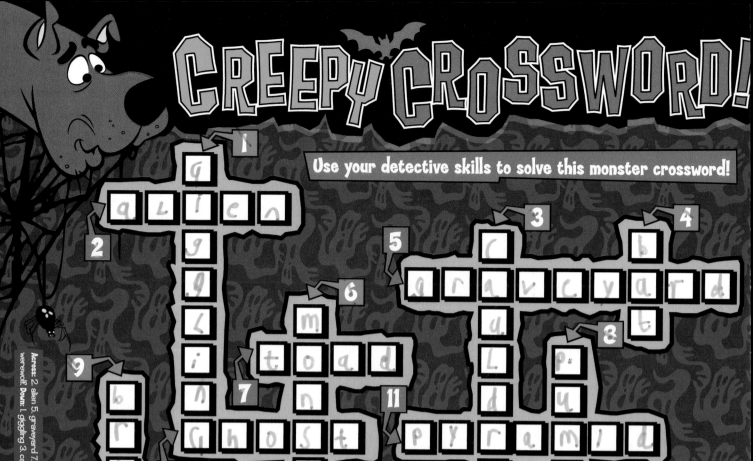

CLUES!

ACROSS

2. Outer space spook (5)
5. Spooky place filled with tombstones (9)
7. Frog-like creature (4)
10. Supernatural being that wears a sheet and says 'Wooo!' (5)
11. Pointy building where mummies are buried (7)
12. Rattling collection of bones (8)
14. It lights the night sky (4)
15. Creepy crawly that spins webs (6)
16. The first villain that the gang encountered was the ------ Knight (5)
18. Howling horror that's half human, half wolf (8)

DOWN

1. Mystery, Inc. took on the -------- Green Ghost (8)
3. Witches mix their spells in these (9)
4. Spooky creature with wings that only comes out at night (3)
6. You'll find one of these living in Loch Ness (7)
8. This orange fruit is used as a lantern on Hallowe'en (7)
9. A witch travels on one of these (5)
12. Slimy creature that slithers along the ground (5)
13. This creepy Count likes the taste of blood (7)
17. Another name for Big Foot (4)

WAT A SCARE!

BRIAN SWENLIN-WRITER
JOE STATON-PENCILLER
DAN DAVIS-INKER
NICK J. NAP-LETTERER
HEROIC AGE-COLORIST
HARVEY RICHARDS-ASST EDITOR
JOAN HILTY-EDITOR

DCSD255

RELAX, SHAGGY-- PEOPLE HAVE BEEN EXPLORING THESE RUINS FOR YEARS AND NOTHING *BAD* HAS EVER HAPPENED...

OH YEAH? LIKE, TELL THAT TO *THEM!*

RULP!

WHOA! HOW DID THAT *BOAT* GET UP THERE?

IT WAS *MERU,* MAN! MERU!

ROH NO! RERU!!

WELL, THAT'S ENOUGH SIGHTSEEING FOR ME. THE CRAB PUFFS ARE A-CALLIN'!

HANG ON, GUYS!

THIS IS SO GROOVY!

OH, HOW BEAUTIFUL-- THESE LOOK LIKE THE RARE ORCHIDS IN YOUR TOUR BOOK.

YOU'RE RIGHT-- THEY'RE AN ENDANGERED FLOWER, PROTECTED BY NATIONAL LAW.

LIKE, THAT'S NOT THE ONLY THING PROTECTING THEM...! L-L-LOOK!

RUT-ROH!

RAAARRRRR!

MERU!

RERU!

CONTINUED ON PAGE 42

SPOT SCOOBY!

The gang are investigating a mystery at a Water Park but they have all got lost! Use your detective skills to find each member of the gang - and keep your eyes peeled for a couple of ghostly villains along the way!

MYSTERY, INC. CHECKLIST

SCOOBY-DOO

VELMA

FRED

SHAGGY

DAPHNE

CREEPY CROOK

GHOSTLY GHOUL

40

LOOK AGAIN!

Take another look at the scene and see if you can spot: a hot dog, a pair of roller skates, a pink striped beach ball, a red baseball cap, a bag of potato chips.

41

RUN, SCOOB! **RUN!**

RI'M RUNNING! RI'M RUNNING!

ZOINKS!

RANG ON, RAGGY!

DEAD END, SCOOB...

≠WHEW!≠

RAAAARRRR

AND I MEAN, LIKE, REALLY *DEAD!*

R'OH NO!

IT LOOKS LIKE WE *LOST* HIM...

...AND *FOUND* SOME SORT OF *STOREROOM.* WHAT ARE EMPTY *PICNIC COOLERS* AND *GARDENING EQUIPMENT* DOING IN *ANGKOR WAT?*

MORE IMPORTANT, WHERE ARE *SHAGGY* AND *SCOOBY?*

PLANT FOOD

LIKE, *GERONIMO!!!*

A HYDROFOIL!

I GET THE FEELING THAT THERE'S MORE TO OUR MONSTER MERU THAN MEETS THE EYE.

DOES SHAGGY KNOW HOW TO DRIVE THAT THING?

LOOK OUT!

RAAARR!!

≈EEP!≈

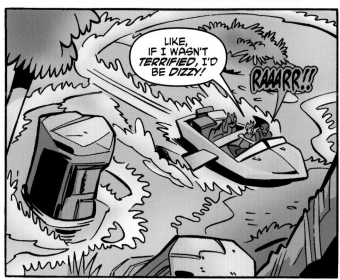

LIKE, IF I WASN'T TERRIFIED, I'D BE DIZZY!

RAAARR!!

ZOINKS! LAND HO!

ROH NO!

≈GASP!≈

CRASH

LIKE, WHO PACKS POSIES FOR A PICNIC?

THOSE AREN'T POSIES—THEY'RE ORCHIDS!

AND IF MY SUSPICIONS ARE CORRECT, THIS *MERU* ISN'T AN *ANCIENT GUARDIAN* AT ALL...BUT A *MODERN THIEF!*

OUR GUIDE, *YAMA!*

LIKE, I DON'T GET IT!

WHEN YAMA REALIZED HOW MUCH *MONEY* HE COULD MAKE SELLING ENDANGERED ORCHIDS, HE USED A COSTUME TO *STIR UP* THE ANCIENT LEGEND OF *MERU*, KEEPING PEOPLE AWAY FROM HIS ILLEGAL FLOWER FARMING!

HE RIGGED THE *BOAT* IN THE *TREE* TO SCARE OFF THE LOCALS, AND TRANSPORTED THE STOLEN ORCHIDS IN THE *PICNIC COOLERS* OF HIS HIDDEN HYDROFOIL.

MY PLAN WAS WORKING, TOO-- I WOULD HAVE BEEN *RICH* IF IT HADN'T BEEN FOR YOU *MEDDLING TOURISTS!*

SO NOW THAT WE'VE SOLVED THAT MYSTERY, CAN WE GET BACK TO OUR *VACATION?*

LOOKS LIKE SCOOBY HAS *ALREADY* STARTED!

ROOBY ROOBY ROO!

HAHAHAHAHAHAHAHAHAHAHAHAHAHAHAHAHAHAHAHAHA The End

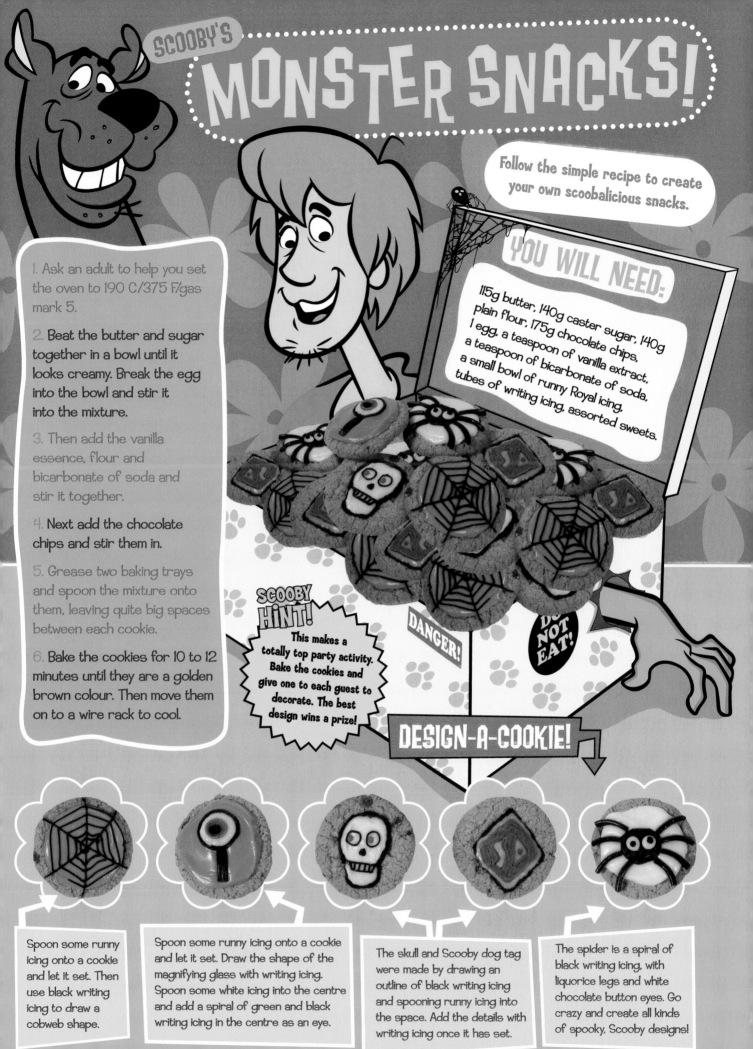

SCOOBY'S MONSTER SNACKS!

Follow the simple recipe to create your own scoobalicious snacks.

YOU WILL NEED:

115g butter, 140g caster sugar, 140g plain flour, 175g chocolate chips, 1 egg, a teaspoon of vanilla extract, a teaspoon of bicarbonate of soda, a small bowl of runny Royal icing, tubes of writing icing, assorted sweets.

1. Ask an adult to help you set the oven to 190 C/375 F/gas mark 5.

2. Beat the butter and sugar together in a bowl until it looks creamy. Break the egg into the bowl and stir it into the mixture.

3. Then add the vanilla essence, flour and bicarbonate of soda and stir it together.

4. Next add the chocolate chips and stir them in.

5. Grease two baking trays and spoon the mixture onto them, leaving quite big spaces between each cookie.

6. Bake the cookies for 10 to 12 minutes until they are a golden brown colour. Then move them on to a wire rack to cool.

SCOOBY HINT!

This makes a totally top party activity. Bake the cookies and give one to each guest to decorate. The best design wins a prize!

DANGER!

DO NOT EAT!

DESIGN-A-COOKIE!

Spoon some runny icing onto a cookie and let it set. Then use black writing icing to draw a cobweb shape.

Spoon some runny icing onto a cookie and let it set. Draw the shape of the magnifying glass with writing icing. Spoon some white icing into the centre and add a spiral of green and black writing icing in the centre as an eye.

The skull and Scooby dog tag were made by drawing an outline of black writing icing and spooning runny icing into the space. Add the details with writing icing once it has set.

The spider is a spiral of black writing icing, with liquorice legs and white chocolate button eyes. Go crazy and create all kinds of spooky, Scooby designs!

I'M GLAD YOU KIDS COULD MAKE IT UP HERE FOR OUR TRICENTENNIAL LOBSTER FESTIVAL!

SO ARE WE, UNCLE WILLIAM. IT'S TOO BAD THAT AUNT GLENDA COULDN'T BE IN TOWN FOR THE FESTIVAL!

YES, SHE LOVES THE FESTIVAL, BUT HER SISTER NEEDED SOME HELP IN VERMONT.

THIS WILL BE SUCH A NICE CHANGE OF PACE FROM GHOST HUNTING!

AND A CHANCE TO EAT SOME GREAT FOOD!

MMM... ROBSTER!

DCSD252

WELL, DAPHNE, YOU WON'T HAVE TO DO ANY GHOST HUNTING HERE, BECAUSE ALL OF OUR GHOSTS ARE FRIENDLY.

HUH?

OOPS. MAYBE I DID FORGET TO MENTION HOW *INTO* GHOSTS THEY ARE HERE...

WE FOLKS OF LIGHTHOUSE HARBOR CHERISH OUR PAST — AND THE GHOSTS THAT COME WITH IT. WE BELIEVE SPIRITS ARE ALL AROUND US — AND THEY'RE LIKE FAMILY!

G-G-GHOSTS?! *EVERYWHERE?!* OHHHH...

ROINKS!

EASY THERE, SHAGGY! IT'S JUST THE LOCALS BELIEVING WHAT THEY WANT TO. YOU DON'T ACTUALLY *SEE* ANY GHOSTS, RIGHT?

LIKE, I DON'T KNOW! I'M NOT GONNA *LOOK!*

NOW I'M LOOKING!

ROW RABOUT A ROOBY RACK?

WHAT A GREAT TURNOUT FOR THE FESTIVAL! THIS TOWN HAS NEVER LOOKED BETTER... AND WE BELIEVE ALL OF OUR FOREFATHERS AND FOREMOTHERS ARE HERE CELEBRATING WITH US!

OOOGAH

GO, BILL-- SOUND THE HORN!

WOO-HOOO!

OH, DON'T WORRY. MY FRIEND HERE WON'T BITE-- HE'S GOT NO *TEETH!* HEH HEH HEH!

ZOINKS! LIKE, THIS "GHOSTS IN THE FAMILY" THING IS TAKING IMAGINARY FRIENDS *TOO FAR!*

MARIE LAPLAQUE! MARIE LAPLAQUE! MARIE LAPLAQUE! ♪ ♪

HEY!

IT'S THOSE TROUBLEMAKING COLLEGE STUDENTS WITH THEIR *CURSED FAN CLUB!*

YOU FOOLS! THAT NAME IS *FORBIDDEN* HERE!

YOU'RE FOLLOWERS OF THE WOMAN WHO *CURSED* THIS TOWN!

MARIE LAPLAQUE IS PART OF THIS TOWN'S *PROUD LEGACY!*

WE WANT THE *TRUTH* TO BE KNOWN!

Curse of the Irate Pirate

AND HERE I BE! I'VE COME FOR ME DUE!

IF YE DO NOT HEED ME, YER PRECIOUS LOBSTER BEDS SHALL BE RUINED AND I'LL FLOOD YER TOWN!

OH NO! MARIE LAPLAQUE!

JINKIES!

ZOINKS! THAT DOESN'T LOOK LIKE A FRIENDLY G-G-GHOST!

ROBBIE BUSCH-WRITER **JOE STATON**-PENCILLER **ANDREW PEPOY**-INKER
PAT BROSSEAU-LETTERER HEROIC AGE-COLORIST HARVEY RICHARDS-ASST EDITOR
JOAN HILTY-EDITOR

LOOK OUT!

YIKES!

MOVE!

HERE SHE COMES!

THE TRUTH SHALL BE KNOWN!

CALM DOWN, EVERYONE! *PLEASE!*

MAYOR, WHAT DOES THIS *MEAN?*

YOU'VE GOTTA *STOP HER,* BILL!

UNCLE WILLIAM... ARE YOU OKAY?

WHAT WAS THAT ALL ABOUT?

IT SEEMS AN OLD TOWN LEGEND'S COME BACK... WITH A *VENGEANCE!*

MARIE LAPLAQUE WAS ALMOST THE *RUINATION* OF THIS TOWN AT ITS BIRTH!

MARIE LAPLAQUE WAS ONE OF THE *FOUNDERS* OF THIS TOWN, WHETHER WE LIKE IT OR NOT. SHE MAY HAVE BEEN A RUTHLESS PIRATE CAPTAIN, BUT HER CREW MUTINIED, BECAUSE SHE WANTED TO STAY AND FIGHT THE BRITISH.

SHE ONLY WANTED TO FIGHT THE BRITS TO PLUNDER OUR WEALTH FOR *HERSELF!* SHE WAS A HEARTLESS WENCH, AND BEFORE THEY MADE HER WALK THE PLANK, SHE *CURSED* THIS TOWN!

HER NAME HAS BEEN *FORBIDDEN* EVER SINCE!

WE CAN GET TO THE BOTTOM OF THIS, UNCLE WILLIAM.

LIKE, THERE GOES OUR VACATION!

I DON'T WANT TO DRAG YOU KIDS INTO THIS...

YOU KIDS THINK YOU CAN SEND THAT SHE-DEVIL BACK TO THE BLACK DEPTHS? OUR ANCESTORS WILL BE MIGHTY UPSET WITH US IF YOU CAN'T!

IT'S OKAY, SIR. IF WE HAVE EVERYONE'S COOPERATION, WE CAN GET TO THE BOTTOM OF THIS.

LET'S SPLIT UP, GANG. SHAGGY AND SCOOBY, COME WITH ME TO CHECK THE HARBOR.

MAYBE I SHOULD GO WITH YOU. THE SAILORS CAN BE A LITTLE *GRUFF* WITH OUTSIDERS.

GRUFF SAILORS ARE BETTER THAN *ANGRY GHOSTS* ANY DAY!

REAH!

I'LL GO WITH THE MARIE LAPLAQUE FAN CLUB TO SEE WHAT I CAN FIND OUT AT THEIR UNIVERSITY. I'LL BET IT'S GOT A FASCINATING LIBRARY!

AND I'LL DIG UP A FEW CLUES HERE IN TOWN.

LET'S MEET BACK HERE IN TWO HOURS.

CHECK!

CHECK!

TANYA AND I WERE DOING RESEARCH LAST WEEK WHEN WE STUMBLED ON THIS--MARIE LAPLAQUE'S *DIARY!*

WHY WAS IT KEPT SECRET FOR SO LONG?

I'VE GOT A COUPLE OF THEORIES ABOUT THAT. IT'S HARD TO KNOW FOR SURE, THOUGH, BECAUSE THERE'S NO RECORD OF WHERE THE DIARY CAME FROM.

RARE BOOKS

I DON'T THINK THIS TOWN WOULD ACCEPT THE TRUTH IF IT SMACKED THEM ON THE NOSE!

IT SEEMS LIKE THEY'VE JUST *GOTTEN* THEIR NOSE SMACKED.

YEAH, WELL, WE'LL SEE HOW THEY DEAL WITH IT!

THE DIARY CAN'T BE TAKEN FROM THE LIBRARY--BUT READ IT AND YOU'LL SEE THE *TRUTH.*

HMM... THIS IS VERY INTERESTING. CAN YOU COME BACK FOR ME IN AN HOUR?

NO PROBLEMO!

MEANWHILE, AT TOWN HALL...

THEN THE OLD WITCH OF THE WOODS CAPTURED THE HUNTER...

UM... HELLO?

...IN HIS OWN TRAP!

YIKES!!!

HI!

AAAAHHHHH!!! THE WITCH!!!

SORRY, KIDS, I WAS JUST LOOKING FOR CLUES. THAT SOUNDED LIKE A *SCARY* GHOST STORY.

IT WAS A REAL STORY!

THE GHOST OF LULU'S GREAT-GRANDPA TOLD IT TO HER!

CONTINUED ON PAGE 55

BATTLE OF THE BADDIES

Mystery, Inc. have met millions of moaning monsters but which ones were the scariest? Check out the official Mystery, Inc. countdown of creepy crooks!

OFFICIAL MYSTERY, INC...
CREEPY CROOKS COUNTDOWN!

ON OFF

5. Zoinks! It's a Zombie!

Like, zombies are guaranteed to turn your knees to jelly! Known as The Living Dead, these freaky creeps wander around with outstretched arms and a glazed expression, looking for spooky fun.

4. You must be batty!

Grab your garlic because at number 4, it's the dreaded Count Dracula! This blood-sucking baddie has caused all kinds of spooky trouble for Scooby and the gang. Daphne is especially scared of his bats because they always get caught in her hair! Jeepers!

3. It's a wrap

Manky mummies always mean trouble! One of the gang's trickiest cases was when they went on the trail of a huge, 2000 year old mummy who could turn its victims to stone. Spooky-Doo!

2. What a ghoul wants

The gang have taken on all kinds of ghouls but one of the most terrifying was the Giggling Green Ghost. Its eerie giggle sent shivers down Scooby's spine and the gang had a tricky time unmasking this freaky fake.

1. The Grim Creeper

Taking the title for 'Best Baddie' is The Creeper. This mean, green creeping machine is terrifying. He has a devious criminal mind, a chilling monster voice and, according to Shaggy, he's got really stinky breath too - everything you need to make a master villain!

5
4
3
2
1

BEST BADDIE

DING! DING! DING!

WINNER!

54

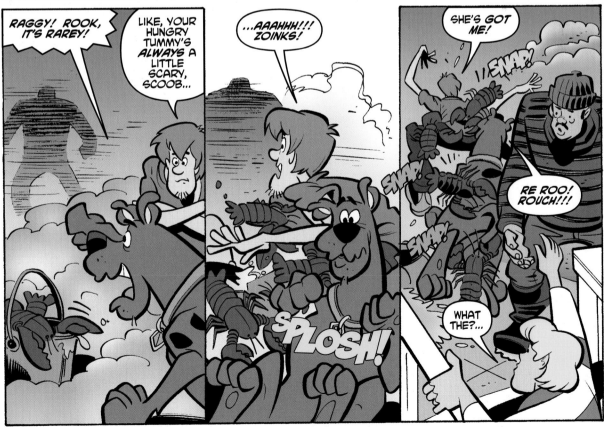

55

REALLY, WE GET IT-- RIGHT, SCOOB?

R-R- RIGHT... RIKES!

NOT YOU TOO...

...AAAAAHHHH!!!

YOU CAN'T RUN FROM THE TRUTH!

DUCK, SCOOB!

YEOW!

HEY?!

!!

UNH! ALMOST GOT HER!

CRAB

GIT YE'SELVES OUT BEFORE THE TRUTH OF THIS TOWN BURIES YE!

KIDS! ARE YOU OKAY?

OOF! SURE SEEMS LIKE WE'RE THE CATCH OF THE DAY!

MAYBE YOU KIDS SHOULD LEAVE THIS FOR THE TOWN TO DEAL WITH. I DON'T WANT YOU TO GET HURT!

BUT WHY WOULD SHE WANT US TO LEAVE, WHEN WE'RE THE ONES TRYING TO HELP THE TOWN ACCEPT HER?

SOMETHING SURE IS *FISHY* ABOUT THAT GHOST.

REAH! AND ROBSTERY ROO!

HMM... I THINK IT'S TIME WE CALLED A *TOWN MEETING!*

PLEASE, EVERYONE, SETTLE DOWN. FREDDIE AND HIS FRIENDS HAVE SOMETHING TO TELL US.

THIS IS THE *DIARY OF MARIE LAPLAQUE.* IT WAS AUTHENTICATED AT THE UNIVERSITY.

OOOOOOOO!!!

THIS PROVES THAT SHE *DIDN'T* DROWN IN THE HARBOR, BUT IN FACT MADE IT BACK TO SHORE AND LIVED QUIETLY IN THE WOODS FOR THE REST OF HER LIFE--*WITH HER SON!*

THAT WITCH HAD NO SON! IT'S A BUNCH OF *LIES!*

HOLD IT NOW, FOLKS...

IT AIN'T *POSSIBLE!*

THE WITCH WALKED THE PLANK!

PLEASE, EVERYONE...

THIS IS A *CROCK!*

PLEASE! THINK ABOUT YOUR *OWN* STORIES -- THE ONES YOU'VE PASSED DOWN TO YOUR CHILDREN.

ESPECIALLY THE ONE ABOUT THE OLD WITCH IN THE WOODS!

THAT ONE'S TRUE, MY GREAT-GREAT-GREAT GRANDPA SWORE IT WAS.

YEAH, MINE TOO.

WELL -- WHAT IF SHE WAS THE *REAL MARIE LAPLAQUE?*

WAIT A MINUTE! VELMA, LET ME SEE THAT DIARY!

SURE.

THIS FLOWER PRESSED BETWEEN THE PAGES... IT LOOKS *FAMILIAR.*

NOOOO! IT'S MINE!

LOOK OUT! THE GHOST'S BACK!

RRIPP!

DON'T LET HER GET THE DIARY!

OOF!

WATCH IT!

HEY!

LOOK OUT!

NOW, LET'S SEE WHO THIS IMPOSTOR IS!

WAIT, FREDDIE!

AUNT GLENDA?!

SORRY DEAR – IT WAS THE LAST CHANCE TO SPARE YOU FROM THE WRATH OF THIS TOWN!

IT'S ALL RIGHT, HONEY. I THINK WE CAN TELL THEM THE TRUTH NOW. THAT FLOWER WAS MARIE'S *FAMILY CREST*...

AND IT'S *MY* CREST TOO. WE FISHERMEN OF THIS TOWN ARE ALL THE *DIRECT DESCENDANTS* OF MARIE. WHEN HER SON CAME BACK TO TOWN, HE CHANGED HIS NAME. THAT MAN WAS MY *GREAT-GREAT-GREAT GRANDFATHER!*

SEE, THE TOWN IS MORE ACCEPTING THAN YOU THOUGHT.

I JUST WANTED TO SLIP THE DIARY INTO THE SCHOOL LIBRARY QUIETLY, SO THAT THE REAL HISTORY OF THE TOWN WOULD COME OUT.

AND I DECIDED TO DRESS UP LIKE MARIE TO SHOCK THE TOWN INTO BE-LIEVING IT.

YEEEE-OOOOW!!!

HA HA HA HA HA HA HA HA

BETTER LOOK OUT, SHAGGY! SCOOBY'S *LOBSTER ROLL* SEEMS TO COME WITH ITS OWN *SECURITY DEVICE!*

SNAP!

THE END

GROOVYSCOPES!

Join the gang for a sneaky peek into what the future might have in store for you! Sounds kinda spooky!

Aquarius (20 January-19 February)
Daphne says: Well Aquarians, it's time for you to get assertive! Sometimes people boss you around and that's so not the look you should go for. Head up, shoulders back and tell them who's boss!

Pisces (20 February-20 March)
Fred says: Well, I can see some great things ahead for you, maybe even a big party! Make the most of it and have a swell time!

Aries (21 March-20 April)
Velma says: Hmm, my tea leaves tell me that there is a great big mystery lined up for you! It's exciting and you'll enjoy solving it. Give the gang a shout if you need a hand!

Taurus (21 April-21 May)
Shaggy says: Like, woah! Kick back and relax, man! Things have been a bit crazy-dazy lately but don't panic. Grab yourself a beanbag, a slice of pizza and snooooooze! Like, I'm feeling better already, dude!

Gemini (22 May-22 June)
Daphne says: If you have fallen out with a friend, now is the time to make up. Arguments are soo last year! Friends are too important to loose - unless they are a tar monster, then you can do without them!

Cancer (23 June-23 July)
Fred says: You have got bags of energy at the moment! A great way to burn it off is by chasing ghouls around haunted houses. If your house isn't haunted, try running in a circle 10 times, that should do the trick!

Leo (24 July-23 August)
Velma says: Your brain is on top form at the moment! Use it wisely and get your homework out of the way. Sounds boring but it pays off in the end!

Virgo (24 August-23 September)
Shaggy says: Like, I'm hungry! Fix me a tower sandwich with chilli chips on the side and you'll have a great day! Cos when you do something nice for someone, you always feel fab!

Libra (24 September-23 October)
Daphne says: The moon is in your sign and it is saying 'Beware of werewolves!'. Look out for them because they always mean trouble, plus they never wash and are really stinky! Ewww!

Scorpio (24 October-22 November)
Fred says: You are full of great ideas at the moment! Make sure you put them to good use. How about inventing a monster catching machine - that always does the trick for me!

Sagittarius (23 November-22 December)
Shaggy says: My mystic crystal ball sees something scary happening on October 31st this year. Witches... ghosts... toffee apples...hey! It must be a Hallowe'en party, how d'ye like that?

Capricorn (23 December-19 January)
Scooby says: Reat rots of rizza. Rand some Rooby Racks. Ren a rilkshake. Raybe some rice cream. Rinish rith a randwich. Rhen sleep! Mm-mmm! Ree-hee-hee! Zzzzzz!

61